The Olden Time Series - Volume III

HENRY MASON BROOKS

1886

TABLE OF CONTENTS

NEW-ENGLAND SUNDAY

Seeing in an old paper that General Washington was stopped by a "tythingman" in Connecticut in 1789 for the "crime" of riding on Sunday, we were naturally led to think about the "Sabbath question," as it is sometimes called. We find the account referred to in the "Columbian Centinel" for December, 1789.

THE PRESIDENT AND THE TYTHINGMAN

The President, on his return to New-York from his late tour, through Connecticut, having missed his way on Saturday, was obliged to ride a few miles on Sunday morning, in order to gain the town, at which he had previously proposed to have attended divine service.—Before he arrived, however, he was met by a Tythingman, who commanding him to stop, demanded the occasion of his riding; and it was not until the President had informed him of every circumstance, and promised to go no further than the town intended, that the Tythingman would permit him to proceed on his journey.

This Sunday question has been so often discussed of late years, and the opinions expressed on the same are so diverse, that it may be well to print a few selections on the subject from some of the old newspapers, that those who are interested may see, as a matter of curiosity, if for no other reason, what views have been entertained within the past century, more especially in New England, in reference to Sunday.

In a Salem paper of 1775 the following notice appeared:—

Whereas the sober and thoughtful People of this Town are much displeased by the great Noise and Disturbance made in the Streets, on Saturday and Sabbath Day Evenings. It is earnestly desired that all Heads of Families would keep their Children and Servants at Home, on those Evenings, and thereby greatly contribute to the Quiet of the Town and Peace of the Inhabitants.

The appearance of Essex Street in Salem at the present time on Saturday evening would seem to indicate that "heads of families" do not now "keep their children and servants at home."

From a communication in the "Massachusetts Centinel," April 30, 1788, "riding on the Sunday" is held to be a "flagrant crime."

For the CENTINEL.

As the devoting one day in seven to religious purposes is a bounden duty we owe to God our creator, and a most reasonable law of our Commonwealth—to see people riding on the Sunday in pursuit of their worldly affairs, is so disgusting to the man of true principle, that the neglect of our executive authority of so flagrant a crime, is to be lamented. The common practice of a Mr. C——fl——n of H-pk——n is notorious on this account. Would not wish to traduce the character of any man, but would only query, whether such conduct is not highly reprehensible, and deserving the cognizance of the magistrate.

Suffolk.

This is not at all strange from the point of view from which Sunday was then regarded. Indeed many people feel about the same now. They would have the old laws enforced in regard to riding and neglect of public worship. They have fears that the day may degenerate into a European Sunday, with prayers in the morning and amusements in the afternoon and evening.

The changes in the past fifty years in reference to Sunday have indeed been very great, but we think they arise chiefly from a reaction from the too strict Puritanism of the past. While we would not have the day too strictly kept, we yet have no sympathy with that class of minds who think there should be no "day of rest" or no time set apart for religious exercises or church services, but would have all days exactly alike.

According to the "Salem Mercury" of Aug. 12, 1788, the ministers of Connecticut, in convention, publish an address on the "increasing negligence of the Publick Worship of God," etc.

SALEM, August 12.

The Ministers of the State of Connecticut, convened in General Association, have published a serious, sensible, plain Address to the People of the Churches and Societies under their pastoral care, on the subject of the increasing negligence of the Publick Worship of God; which they consider as one of the most painful and alarming, among the various instances of declension and immorality, which at the present time threaten the very existence of religion in this country.—"In what manner," says the Address, "does this evil affect the political interests, the essential wellbeing, of the community? All the branches of morality are indissolubly connected. From one breach of moral obligation to a second, to a third, and to all, the transition is easy, necessary and rapid. From negligence of the duties we owe to God, the passage is short to contempt for those we owe to men. The Sabbath, in the judgment of reason and of revelation, is the great hinge on which all these duties are turned. When the ordinances of this holy day are forsaken and forgotten, the whole system of moral obligation must of course be also forgotten; the great, substantial and permanent good, of which religion is the only source, is effectually destroyed; the political peace and welfare of a community, the salvation of the human soul, the infinitely benevolent designs of redeeming love, the institution of the means of grace, and the obedience and sufferings of the Son of God, are frustrated and set at nought. Thus, by one effectual blow of sin, and the friends of sin, are all the great and valuable interests of mankind overthrown."

Although our remarks are confined to America, we may mention that it has been stated by some of our own countrymen who have visited London that Sunday is generally as well observed there as in New England; yet we find in the "Salem Gazette" of Nov. 23, 1785, that the attendance on public worship in London was then rather small as compared with what might have been seen in Boston at the same date. But that was before the days of the "sensation" preachers, as they are called,—Spurgeon, Beecher, Talmage, and men of that stamp, who now draw crowds of people, many of whom are not always the most religious in the community, but who love excitement rather than quiet contemplation.

LONDON,

Sept. 13. Sunday being a day of rest, 739 horses were yesterday engaged on parties of pleasure.

In fifty churches, eastward of Temple-bar, the congregations amounted, on an average, to seven for each church in the morning, and five in the afternoon. This shews the state of the Christian religion in the metropolis to be far better than could be expected!

1785.

The following extract from the "Belfast Patriot" of 1825 shows how the "Lord's day" was regarded in 1776 in the "District of Maine."

Fifty Years Ago. At a town meeting, held on the common, on the south end of lot No. 26, probably where the meeting house now stands, on the east side of the river, in Belfast, Oct. 10th, 1776, the town then having been incorporated two years—among other things "to see if there can be any plan laid to stop the Inhabitants from visiting on Sunday." "Voted, That if any person makes unnecessary vizits on the Sabeth they shall be Lookt on with Contempt untill they make acknowledgement to the Public."

Houses of worship were formerly "as cold as a barn."

Notwithstanding all the comforts and conveniences of modern places of worship, to say nothing about the more interesting preaching and other exercises, some people consider it a hardship to be obliged to attend even one service on Sunday. How was it in "old times"? Our ancestors were obliged to conform to the prevalent custom of going to meeting whether they liked it or not. The law did not then excuse any one from attendance at public worship, except for sickness. Not to be a "meeting-goer" in those days was to range one's self with thieves and robbers and other outlaws. No matter if the meeting-house was cold, and there was danger of consumption; it was apparently "more pleasing to the Lord" that a man should get sick attending services in "his house" than by staying away preserve his health. Mr. Felt, in his "Annals of Salem," says: "For a long period the people of our country did not consider that a comfortable degree of warmth while at public worship contributed much to a profitable hearing of the gospel. The first stove we have heard of in Massachusetts for a meeting-house was put up by the First congregation of Boston in 1773. In Salem the Friends' Society had two plate-stoves brought from Philadelphia in 1793. The North Church had one in 1809; the South had a brick Russian stove in 1812. About the same date the First Church had a stove and the Tabernacle had one also. The objections that [to heat churches] was contrary to the custom of their hardy fathers and mothers, [and that it] was an indication of extravagance and degeneracy, had ceased to be advanced. Not a few remember the general knocking of feet on cold days and near the close of long sermons. On such occasions the Rev. Dr. Hopkins used to say, now and then: 'My hearers, have a little patience, and I will soon close.'" Mr. Felt says that Hugh Peters (one of the ministers of the First Church) was represented by an English painter as in a pulpit with a large assembly before him, turning an hour-glass and using these words: "I know you are good fellows, stay and take another glass."

The Lord's Day in Connecticut in 1788.

ANECDOTE.

A Gentleman in the State of Connecticut, regularly attended publick worship on the Lord's day with all his family: On the Sunday evening he always catechised his children and servants on the principles of religion, and what they heard the minister deliver from the pulpit. He had a negro man who never could remember a note of the sermon, though otherwise smart. At last his master peremptorily told him he would on Monday morning tie him up and flog him. Next Sunday evening, when interrogated, he had forgotten all: On Monday morning his master executes his threat so far, as to tie him up. The fellow then cried out, O master spare me, for I remember something the minister said. What is it? said the master. The fellow replied, "This much may suffice at this time." His master was so pleased with his wit that he forgave him.

Salem Mercury, August 12.

From the Rev. Dr. Bentley's notes, edited by Stanley Waters, printed in the "Salem Gazette," we learn that even in old times people occasionally absented themselves from public worship on the Lord's Day.

Under date of 1791 we read,—

Jan. 23. No singing through the whole day—not even an attempt. Mr. Le Favre Swan and Parker promised their assistance, but by drawing a prize of £300 in the Lottery they have been detained from Public Worship.

And in 1792,—

Mch. 11. Sunday. The Ship Grand Turk burdened 550 Tons sailed this day for India, Capt. B. Hodges.

The previous invitations given to the principal Gentlemen of the Town and the fame of a ship built in the Town and furnished with Sails from our own manufactories urged a curiosity so strong that few people were left in our houses of worship. Weather fine.

Thus we see that pecuniary success and pleasant weather were as influential in 1792 as they are in 1886 in diverting individuals from their ordinary religious privileges.

The following extracts from the "Salem Impartial Register" of July 27, 1801, will perhaps have interest when considered in connection with some circumstances which have taken place in Salem within a year or two:—

THE CONNECTICUT SABBATH.

IN ancient days, 't was God's most sacred will,
To give his law on Sinai's lofty hill,
Whose top terrific issued clouds of smoke,
And thus, amidst the flames, th' Eternal spoke;
Six days, said he, (and loud the same express'd)
Shall men still labor, and on the seventh rest:
But here alas! like yon great pious town,[A]
They break his law, and thus prefer their own:
"And let it be enacted further still,
That all our people strict observe our will:
Five days and half shall men and women too
Attend their business, and their mirth pursue.
But after that, no man without a fine,
Shall walk the streets, or at a tavern dine.
One day and half 'tis requisite to rest,
From toilsome labor, and a tempting feast.
Henceforth let none, on peril of their lives,
Attempt a journey, or embrace their wives:
No Barber, foreign or domestic bred,
Shall e'er presume to dress a lady's head.
No shop shall spare (half the preceding day),
A yard of Ribband, or an ounce of Tea.
Five days and half th' inhabitants may ride
All round the town, and villages beside;
But, in their travels, should they miss the road,
'Tis our command they lodge that night abroad."
From hence 'tis plainly seen how chang'd indeed,
That sacred law which GOD himself decreed!
In this one act they think to merit heav'n,
By taking half a day from six to add to seven.

[A] Boston—where a similar law was formerly enforced with rigour.

"One Man esteemeth one day above another; another esteemeth every day ALIKE. Let every man be fully persuaded in his own mind."
Romans xiv. 5.

The old custom of opening Barbers' Shops in this Town on Sunday ceased yesterday, in consequence of the determination of the Grand Jury to make presentment of all such violations of the Sabbath. Cautions have also been given to the Horse Letters, against loaning any Horses or Carriages on Sunday; and there appears to be a very serious and wise determination in the "Gentlemen of the Grand Jury" to put a stop to those shameful practices, which have for twenty years disgraced the most sober and quiet Town in Massachusetts! Laus Deo! There will be no more horses killed now of a Sunday in going to Boston, either by lack of bating, or by hard driving! It is whispered, that the public are indebted, for this salutary reform, to the covert exertions of a ci-devant Preacher, who lacking the ability to lead his wakeful flock formerly, is now determined to drive all within his Circuit, into the pale of obedience, and thereby make up for former Sins of Omission. The Federalists predicted the loss of Religion, should Jefferson be President. We certainly have a good Sample (thus early under his administration) that its state will be improved.

Although doubts have often been expressed as to the authenticity of certain Connecticut "Blue Laws," it is probable that many laws which have sometimes been referred to as such were in the early days of the colony actually in force,—as the following, which we find in an old paper. They are certainly not much stronger than laws of the time in Massachusetts.

No one shall be a freeman, or give a vote, unless he be converted, and a member in full communion, of one of the Churches allowed in this dominion.

No one shall travel, cook victuals, make beds, sweep house, cut hair, or shave, on the Sabbath day.

No woman shall kiss her child on the Sabbath, or fasting-day.

No one shall run on the Sabbath day, or walk in his garden, or elsewhere, except reverently to and from meeting.

No one shall read common prayer books, keep Christmas, or set days, make minced pies, dance, play cards, or play on any instrument of music, except the Drum, Trumpet, or Jewsharp.

No food or lodging shall be offered to a Quaker, Adamite, or other heretic.

If any person turns Quaker, he shall be banished, and not suffered to return but on pain of death.

No Roman Catholic priest shall abide in the dominion; he shall be banished, and suffer death on his return.

Some years ago, a law-book which had belonged to Jonathan Trumbull, containing the early statutes of Connecticut, was in the possession of a Boston gentleman,[1] who informs us that at the end of the volume, in manuscript, were found reports of "Brother Jonathan's" adjudications of small cases which he tried as "justice of the peace." Among them was one where "His Majesty's tythingman" entered a complaint against Jona and Susan Smith for a "profanation of the Sabbath;" namely, "That on the —— day of —— during Divine Service on the Lord's Day they did smile." The culprits were adjudged to be guilty of the offence, and severally fined "five shillings and costs." This book was shown to the late Professor Agassiz, who examined it with great interest and then made the following remark: "I find here evidence of the difference between the Calvinism of Switzerland and the Calvinism of America. I was brought up in that faith. I went to meeting in the morning, I danced with the parson's daughter on the green in the afternoon, and I played whist with the parson in the evening."

[1] Edward Atkinson, Esq.

The legislature of Massachusetts in the year 1760 passed the following laws in relation to Sunday and to the proper observance of Saturday evening:—

"Whereas it is the Duty of all Persons, upon the Lord's-Day carefully to apply themselves publickly and privately to Religion and Piety, the Prophanation of the Lord's-Day is highly offensive to Almighty God; of evil Example and tends to the Grief and Disturbance of all pious and religiously disposed persons.

Therefore that the Prophanation of the said Day may be fully prevented: Be it further enacted, That no Person whatsoever shall keep open their Shops andc. andc.—do or exercise any Labour nor any Sport, Game Play or Recreation on the Lord's Day or any part thereof andc. andc. under penalties of not exceeding twenty shillings for every offence."

Travelling was also prohibited, and it was enacted,—

"That if any Person or Persons shall be recreating, disporting or unnecessarily walking or loitering, or if any Persons shall unnecessarily assemble themselves in any of the Streets, Lanes, Wharves, High-Ways, Commons, Fields, Pastures or Orchards of any Town or Place within this Province upon the Lord's Day, or any Part thereof, every Person so offending shall forfeit and pay the sum of five shillings and upon a second Conviction bound for good behaviour,... If any Persons being able of Body and not otherwise necessarily prevented shall for the space of one Month together absent themselves from the Publick Worship of God on the Lord's Day, they shall forfeit and pay the sum of ten shillings.

"And whereas many Persons are of opinion that the Sabbath or Time of religious Rest, begins on Saturday evening, therefore to prevent all unnecessary Disturbance of Persons of such Opinion, as well as to encourage in all others a due and seasonable Preparation for the religious Duties of the Lord's Day: Be it further enacted, That no Person shall keep open any Shop, Ware-House or Work-House or hawk or sell any Provisions or Wares in Streets or Lanes of any Town or District, or be present at any

Concert of Musick, Dancing or other Publick Diversion on the Evening next preceding the Lord's-Day, on Pain of forfeiting ten Shillings for each Offence, andc."

Wardens were to be appointed in all the towns and districts to see that these laws were duly enforced. All existing laws on the Sabbath were at that time repealed, but some of the laws then passed are still in force.

The following is from Felt's "Annals of Salem:"—

1676.

April 20th. "Ordered by ye Selectmen yt the three Constables doe attend att ye three great doores of ye meeting house every Lord's day att ye end of sermon, boath forenoone and afternoone and to keep ye doors fast and suffer none to goe out before ye whole exercise bee ended, unless itt be such as they conceive have necessary occasion and to take notice of any such as shall presume to goe forth as above said and present their names as ye law directs. Ordered that all ye boys of ye towne are and shall bee appointed to sitt upon ye three paire of staires in ye meeting house on the Lord's day and Wm. Lord is appointed to look to the boyes yt sitt upon ye pulpit staires and for ye other staires Reuben Guppy is to look to and order soe many of ye boyes as may be convenient and if any are unruly to present their names as ye law directs."

On Sundays, P.M. when sermon is ended, the people in the galleries come down and march two abreast up one ile and down another until they come before the desk, for pulpit they have none. Before the desk is a long pue where the Elders and Deacons sit, one of them with a money box in his hand, into which the people as they pass, put their offerings, some 1s., some 2s. or a half crown, or 5s., according to their ability and good will, after this they conclude with a psalm.

While in 1814 in some parts of Massachusetts and New Hampshire the tithingmen felt obliged to issue an address of warning to the public, in Boston in 1815 Sunday seems to have been well observed. We copy two notices from the "Salem Gazette."

To the Public.

As the profanation of the Lord's Day is inconsistent with the welfare of society and a gross violation of the laws of the State; therefore we the undersigned, being appointed Tithingmen, give notice to the public, that we are under oath, and it has become our indispensable duty to prosecute all, who wilfully violate the laws with respect to the Lord's Day.

And we hereby request all persons, to abstain on the Lord's Day from travelling, from worldly business and amusement, and thus relieve us from the painful necessity of prosecuting for a violation of the laws of the State.

[Signed by the Tithingmen of Concord, N.H. Salem, N.H. Bradford, Ms. Andover, Reading, Tewksbury, Beverly, Manchester, Hamilton, Ipswich, and Wilmington.]

Aug. 6, 1814.

BOSTON JUNE 1.—At the meeting on Monday last, the town of Boston evinced its good sense by voting to postpone the choice of Tythingmen till the first Monday of March next. We venture to assert, that in no district in the universe, of the extent and population of Massachusetts, is the Sabbath more decently and sincerely observed.

Law against keeping barber's shops open on Sunday morning in Salem in 1804:—

SUNDAY LAW IN SALEM—BARBERS' SHOPS 80 YEARS AGO.

Correspondence of the Salem Gazette.

Boston, Aug. 5.

About 1804 your Selectmen ordered that after a given date no barber's shop should be kept open on Sunday morning. There was no appeal from their mandate. The fatal last Sunday arrived; the customers of the esteemed Benj. Blanchard, whose shop was at the upper part of Essex street, opposite the Endicott and Cabot mansions, came as usual to have their hair tied; it was the epoch of queues, and it was necessary to their aspect in church that their back hair should be artistically bound with ribbon and their heads nicely pomatumed, even though, like Bonaparte, they shaved their own beards. This last Sunday it was observable that each gentleman, in his turn, after being barbered, instead of hurrying off as usual, resumed his seat. As the second bell began to ring, the last customer was accomplished, and the whole company rose from their chairs, filed out into Essex street, formed a line in front of Mr. Blanchard's shop, and gave three rousing cheers; then, like Burns's "Twa Dogs, each took off his several way," some to Dr. Barnard's North Church, some to Dr. Hopkins's, Dr. Bolles's, or Dr. Prince's First Church.

Salem Gazette, August, 1885.

The Middlesex Sabbath Association meet in November, 1815, but find nothing to do. No Sabbath-breakers reported, probably.

Sabbath Association.

Whereas the Association in the county of Middlesex, for aiding in carrying into effect the Laws of this Commonwealth against the violation of the Sabbath, met at Concord in November last,—and finding nothing which required further proceedings at that time, thought fit to adjourn. This is to give notice, that the meeting of said Association stands adjourned, to meet at Concord, at the former place of meeting, in Hamilton's Hotel, on the first Wednesday in February next, at ten o'clock A.M.

A general attendance is requested.

CHARLES STEARNS, Per Order.

Lincoln, January 11, 1816.

Columbian Centinel.

The following notice from the "Columbian Centinel" shows that rapid

driving on the Lord's Day was forbidden in Boston as lately as 1817:—
POLICE OFFICE.

Boston, July 12, 1817.

Complaints having been made at this office of dangers and disturbances arising from the rapidity with which carriages are driven on the Lord's Day, special persons have been selected to take notice of this indecorous conduct, that the law on the subject may be rigidly enforced. It is forbidden to drive, during Divine Service, or while the inhabitants are going to or returning from their several houses of public worship, any carriage at a greater rate than a walk or moderate foot pace; and masters and mistresses are responsible, if the servants are unable to pay the penalty incurred by them in this offence.

NEH. FREEMAN, Superintendent.

Making hay on Sunday is here condemned in some very choice lines.

☞ There is much more piety than poetry in the following stanzas:—And though the employment condemned, cannot occur for a season at least, the moral inculcated we trust, will have a tendency to prevent other breaches of Holy Time.

THE PIOUS FARMER.

SHOULD it rain all the week and the Sundays prove fine,
Though others make hay, yet I'll not work at mine;
For, I don't think, for my part, such sun-shine was given,
Us mortals to lure from the path-way to heaven.
Some to work on the Sabbath will make a pretence,
That taxes are high, and they can't pay their rents;
But my rents and my taxes I'll still hope to pay,
Though on sun-shiny Sundays I do not make hay.
For this shall my heart never call me a sinner,
While I still hope in God I shall ne'er want my dinner;
To lay up a store, I'd try every fair way,
But on Sundays, though sun shines, I will not make hay.
Some plead in excuse, that, not waiting for Monday,
Great battles are won, though they're fought on a Sunday!
At famed Waterloo too,—there's none greater than it,
But then, 'tis well known, the lost Tyrant began it.
'Tis a custom with me to spend godly that day;
But while French go to war, and the English make hay,
Though the season proves wet, and hay gets in but slowly,
Yet I would not do other than keep the day holy.
Far, far be from me, to ape those saving Elves,
Who rob God of his due, to grow richer themselves;
But be mine the pursuit, which all good men approve,
To strive to be rich in the Regions above.

If it rain all the Week, then on God I'll recline,
And not work on Sunday, although the sun shine:
In this Faith deeply rooted, no ills I forbode,
That a man's seldom poorer for serving his God.
Columbian Centinel, Nov. 27, 1816.

From the "Essex Register," Salem, May 18, 1822, we learn that there had been trouble caused by ill-bred young men congregating at the public corners on Sunday evening, and also that some females had behaved badly at that time.

One of those ill bred and riotous fellows, who have become notorious for their bad conduct of late, at the corners of our streets, was arrested by one of our most vigilant constables, at the corner of North and Essex streets, on Sunday evening last, carried before a magistrate, committed to prison, and bound over for his future good conduct. Our municipal authorities, and all others concerned in bringing this person to punishment, deserve the thanks of their fellow-citizens. The town of Salem, once so distinguished for the purity of its manners and the good order of its society, has been disgraced of late, by outrages upon the peace and quiet of the community, committed by noisy assemblages of young men at the public corners—and even females have been seen to exhibit a demeanor in the streets disreputable to the town, and disgraceful in the highest degree to themselves. This conduct should receive not only the discountenance, but the decided reprehension of the respectable part of the community. Every citizen is interested, and is moreover bound to manifest his interest by his acts, in bringing every offender to prompt and condign punishment. The stake which every one has in the good order of the community, is great—it behoves, then, every one to exert himself to re-establish and preserve it.

In 1819 in New York there were loud complaints of the violation of the Sabbath, as we see by an account taken from the "Salem Gazette."

NEW-YORK, JULY 14.

VIOLATION OF THE SABBATH.

A few weeks since, a meeting of the citizens was called, to devise some efficient means to suppress the violation of the Sabbath. A committee was appointed to report a plan for that purpose. I wish to inquire what that committee have done, and when another meeting is to be called to receive their report.—The evil still remains, and is certainly accumulating under the most aggravated forms.—Our churches are nearly deserted on the Sabbath, while every place of amusement and pleasurable retreat is thronged. Good authority states the numbers that frequent Brooklyn every Sabbath, at from ten to twenty thousand, and a proportionable number may be computed to visit every other island and place of resort in the vicinity. We have forty-five churches, and a population of one hundred and twenty thousand; admitting one thousand to attend each church, it follows that seventy-five thousand violate that command of the Apostle which requires Christians "not to forsake the assembling of themselves together." Let the citizens organize societies to suppress the violation of the Sabbath and all other vice and immorality.

"Sabbath-breakers" had multiplied to such an extent in 1815 that conventions were held in many of the counties in Massachusetts to see what could be done in reference to the evil. We have a report of the Essex convention at Topsfield, Oct. 4, 1815. The Committee say, among other things,—

Although most men, even if they have no regard for the Divine Being or the welfare of society, when they know that Sabbath-breaking is offensive to the great body of the community, will, from regard to themselves, refrain from it, yet there are some abandoned individuals, who are so lost to all proper regard even for themselves, as well as their Maker, and their fellow-men, that in violation of laws, human and Divine, and in direct opposition to the wishes of the community, they still continue to travel and labour upon the Sabbath.

Such persons ought surely to be prosecuted, and made to feel that they cannot violate the laws of the Commonwealth, and profane the Sabbath with impunity.

If their conduct is suffered to continue, others will be emboldened to follow their example; the evil will again increase, and eventually become as great as before.

But if they find that they cannot profane the Sabbath without being subjected to the trouble, shame and expense of a penal prosecution, this enormous evil, which has so long been undermining the best interests of the community, and drawing down upon us Divine judgments, will be prevented. For past experience has fully demonstrated, that wherever the laws are prudently, and at the same time promptly and faithfully executed, the evil will cease.

And among the Resolves passed by the Convention we find these,—

III. Resolved, that we earnestly recommend to Tythingmen, Civil Officers and the friends of the Sabbath in every town, to prosecute, or cause to be prosecuted, without distinction and without delay, all, who are travelling without sufficient reason, or in any way wilfully violating the laws respecting the Lord's Day.

V. Resolved, that we recommend to all the friends of order, to circulate as extensively as possible, such tracts and pamphlets as are calculated to promote the due observance of the Lord's Day.

Voted, that the Clerk be requested to send a copy of the doings of the Convention, to the Editors of the public papers in Boston, Salem, Newburyport and Haverhill, and that they be requested to publish the same in their respective papers.

A full account of this convention can be found in the "Salem Gazette," Oct. 31, 1815. It does not appear that there was any disturbance of public worship to complain of, only many people neglected to attend the meetings, or walked or rode for pleasure on the Lord's Day.

In the same month and year the "Worcester Ægis" gave expression to opinions on the question of "Sabbath-breaking" which we think accord more with modern ideas than do those of the Essex convention. The views of the "Ægis" probably represented the average liberal sentiment of that day.

WORCESTER, OCT. 25.

BREACH OF THE SABBATH.

At the late session of the S.J. Court at Northampton it was decided that a justice of the peace could not issue a warrant for a breach of the Sunday laws against an offender that is not an inhabitant of the county where the offence is committed, but that he must be prosecuted only before a grand jury; and that justices of the peace could not issue warrants, nor sheriffs serve them, on the Lord's day, for any breaches of those laws. Damages were awarded against a justice, a tythingman, and a sheriff, upon the latter principle.

Upon this decision we congratulate the public. It has taken a formidable weapon from the hands of those petty tyrants, who are labouring to revive the reign of religious persecution. We trust we shall no longer see the Sabbath trespassed upon by these official harpies, who, instead of spending the day as they ought, in worshiping God, confessing their own manifold sins, and praying that they may be endued with a more christian temper, are riding or walking the highway, "seeking whom they may devour," and gratifying at once their malice and their avarice, by plundering their fellow-citizens, and filling their own pockets. In some towns they have been stationed at every turn of the road, ready to dart out upon the traveller, like a spider from the corner of his web. We rejoice at every occurrence which checks this persecuting spirit.—Those who know us, know that we respect the Sabbath and its holy institutions: for this very reason we reprobate conduct which has a direct tendency to bring these institutions into contempt. In all ages, the anti-christian spirit of christian professors has done more injury to the cause of religion, than the attacks of its declared enemies. Real Christianity cannot flourish by persecution. Excessive rigour defeats the very purposes it is intended to subserve. In time there will be a re-action, and men will go to the opposite extreme—religion and morals will be as much too lax, as they were before too strict.

In no part of the world is the sabbath so scrupulously observed as in New-England. As we keep it, it resembles more the Jewish Sabbath, than the Sabbath of all other parts of Christendom. We had much rather see this nice punctiliousness, than that indifference which prevails in some places.

But we think there is such a thing as drawing the cord too tight—so tight that it will be in danger of snapping in sunder! The good habits of our countrymen, and the increasing regard which is entertained for religion, will be a sure guaranty of the respectful observance of the Sabbath. There are very few men in the community, who dare to outrage public feeling by a wanton violation of the solemnity of the day. We have excellent laws to punish those who disturb the devotions of any society or individual. Let these laws be put in execution without fear, favour or affection. But for the rest, let religion take care of itself—it needs no assistance from the feeble arm of the magistrate.

Tythingmen's Notice.

We the subscribers, Tythingmen of the several towns annexed to our names, having taken the Oath of Office, it becomes our indispensable duty to see the laws of this Commonwealth, "for the due observation of the Lord's Day," faithfully executed; which we are determined to do as far as may be in our power. We, therefore, call on all persons to abstain from the violation of said laws; as they would avoid "the several penalties annexed to the several offences therein described," and save us from the painful necessity of a prosecution, which otherwise must immediately follow.

DAVID LANE, }
Tithingman of Bedford in
behalf of himself and five
others.

BENJ. OSGOOD, }
Tithingman of Westford
in behalf of himself and
four others.

JOHN JACOBS, }
Tithingman of Carlisle in
behalf of himself and one
other.

SAM'l WHITING, }
Tithingman of Bilerica
in behalf of himself and
nine others.

May 27th, 1815.

Lord's Day.

Notice is hereby given, that the Middlesex Convention for suppressing violations of the Laws of the Commonwealth, relative to the Sabbath, stands adjourned to the third Wednesday in May, at Hamilton's Tavern in Concord, at 10 o'clock, A.M.

JACOB COGGIN, Sec'y.

N. B.—It is particularly requested that all the Clergy, and others in the county, who feel interested in the object would attend.

may 13, 1815

The Sabbath. An ecclesiastical council was lately convened at Kingsbury, N. York, to decide a controversy which had originated between the minority and majority of the Baptist Church, in Kingsbury, respecting an observance of the Christian Sabbath. One of the Elders of the Church, Mr. Culver, had written, preached and published a discourse, which, in the opinion of the Council, amounted to a full and complete denial of all Scriptural authority, for observing a day as a Christian Sabbath. The Council, after stating the reasons, which in their opinion, conclusively proved the obligation of the Christian to observe the Sabbath, recommend an union between the parties to this controversy, and if the majority do not comply, the Council deem it their imperious duty, to recognize the minority as the regular Baptist Church.

In a former paper, we alluded to the manner in which the Sabbath was regarded by our ancestors. It appears, that the following special instructions on this subject were given to Gov. Endicott, by the New-England Plantation Company.

"And to the end, the Saboth may bee celebrated in a religious manner, we appoint, that all that inhabite the plantation, both for the general and particular employment, may surcease their labor, every Satterday throughout the year, at three of the clock in the afternoone, and that they spend the rest of the day in catechising and preparation for the Saboth, as the minister shall direct."

Salem Observer, Aug. 4, 1827.

In the "Salem Register" of Oct. 11, 1820, we find the report of the trial of a man charged with the crime of Sabbath-breaking by delivering milk to his customers. The presiding judge (Mitchell) seems to have made a very sensible address to the jury on this occasion. Probably the surest way to bring about speedily the much-dreaded "European Sunday" would be for some person or persons to prosecute such individuals as they happen to know who violate certain obsolete Sunday laws.

Law Intelligence.

Commonwealth vs. Glover.

This was an appealed case. The justice before whom it was originally tried, imposed a fine on Glover, who appealed to the Common Pleas. It was tried at Dedham on the 21st ult.

The complaint was that said Glover had been guilty of the crime of Sabbath breaking, by delivering milk to his customers in Boston on the 25th June last. The evidence to support the complaint was from two gentlemen, Messrs. M'Clure and Vose. They testified, that on the 25th June last they walked out in company at 5, A.M. to see if they could discover any persons delivering milk from carts—that they had not been long in pursuit, before they descried a man, who descended from his vehicle, with a milk vessel, and poured milk from it, which he delivered to a family in their presence.— They approached him—enquired his name, and from whence he came. He answered, from Quincy, and his name was Glover.—They asked if he was in the habit of bringing milk to Boston on the Sabbath. He told them he had been when the weather was very hot. This was the evidence.

The complaint being for doing labour on the Sabbath in the county of Norfolk, which was not labour of necessity or mercy.

Churchill, for Defendant, in cross examining the witnesses, enquired why they rose at so early an hour, on the 25th June, and went to walk? They answered that it was partly to exercise, and partly to perform their duty as professors of religion. They said they had made up their minds that the moiety of the fines they expected to receive, they would give to some charitable institution.

The defence rested on two points—First, That no crime or act was proved to have been committed in Norfolk county—Secondly, If it should be proved that the act complained of had been committed, it was an act of necessity and mercy.

Counsellor Churchill entered with much spirit into the cause, and evinced that he had bestowed upon it much thought and labour. He gave an elaborate history of the Sabbatical Institution, and stated the various opinions and laws as to the division of holy time. He said that many families in Boston, both poor and rich, depended on milk to feed their children—that a large proportion of the people had no conveniences for keeping it from Saturday night till Monday morning; that those who had no other way of disposing of their milk, but by delivering it to those who would suffer without it, performed an act embracing both necessity and mercy; that those who sat up all night for the purpose of being up before day, to fatten on those who were performing the before-named charitable act, were like the Jews of old, who, when the Saviour of mankind raised the dead and restored the blind to sight, cried out, Crucify him! the Jews were but the M'Clures of the present day.

The Judge (Mitchell) charged the jury, that, if they had doubts whether any offence were proved to have been committed, within the county, they must acquit; or, if otherwise, and they were of opinion that it was necessary to deal out milk on the Sabbath in extreme hot weather, they must acquit. He stated that his neighbours bought milk of him, and took it on Sunday as on other days, and thought it no crime. He did not cast up the score, receive the money and rub out the chalks on that day; but apprehended that his conduct was virtually the same as that charged upon the defendant. The defendant pursued his regular course, and in doing so, he saved his property from waste, and relieved many from disappointment and distress. The clergy ride from town to town on the Sabbath, and the physicians ride without molestation. The Sabbath is a day of rest—but in the exercise of its duties, reason is to be regarded. Such worldly concerns as can well be done on other days, ought not to be done on the Sabbath—but if an ox fall into a pit, he must be taken out; that if a clergyman has agreed to exchange with a brother, he may as well ride a few miles on the Sabbath as to make a parade of going on Saturday night.

The jury returned a verdict of—NOT GUILTY.

Observance of the Sabbath. There has been lately, in some of the Boston papers, a discussion of the question, whether the sailing of a steam boat on the Sabbath is not a profanation.

We allude to this subject, at the present time, not for the purpose of taking a side in the controversy, but merely to show in what manner this day was formerly noticed in England, and our own country.

In England, during the reign of James the first, it was lawful for his subjects to indulge in certain sports, such as dancing, archery, leaping, vaulting, may-games, whitsun ales, and morris dances, on Sunday after evening service. But it was not lawful to have bear-baiting, bull-baiting, interludes, and bowling.

In reign of Charles 1st a statute was passed, prohibiting a meeting out of the parish, on the Lord's day, to enjoy these sports. A statute was afterwards passed, prohibiting carriers and drovers from travelling, and butchers from slaughtering or selling on this day. Afterwards all tradesmen, artificers, workmen, laborers, or other persons, were prohibited from exercising their callings on this day, excepting works of necessity and charity, and dressing and selling meat in families, inns, cook-shops, andc. selling milk before nine in the morning, and after four in the afternoon, selling mackerell before or after divine service, and excepting also forty watermen, who may ply between Vauxhall and Limehouse.

By a statute of George 2d fish carriages were allowed to pass on Sundays, whether laden or empty. During the reign of this King, the Court decided in favor of a Baker, charged "with baking puddings and pies on the Lord's day for dinner." The court considered the case as falling within the exceptions of works of necessity and charity. "That it was better that one baker and his men should stay at home, than many families and servants." Under George 3d Bakers were prohibited from making, baking or selling, excepting between nine in the morning and one in the afternoon, and the person requiring the baking carried or sent it to the place where it was to be baked. A law was afterwards passed, permitting bakers to work, so far as may be necessary in setting or superintending the sponge, to prepare the dough for the next day's baking.

The provisions of the Colony and Province laws, on this subject, were embodied in our State law of 1792, which prohibits every person from keeping open his shop, ware-house, or work-house, on the Lord's day, and from doing any labor or work, excepting that of necessity and charity, and from attending concerts of music, dancing, andc. It likewise prohibits travelling by drovers, teamsters, andc. visiting taverns, andc. during the time included between the midnight preceding and the sun-setting of the Lord's day. It likewise prohibits games, diversions, recreations on the land or water, on the evening next preceding or succeeding the Lord's day. Under the Colonial government, it was for some time made a question when the Sabbath should be considered as commencing; but in 1645 it became a custom to regard the evening of the last day of the week as the beginning of the Sabbath. Several clergymen however considered Saturday afternoon as the commencement of holy time.

The following extracts from our town records will show in what manner the Sabbath was observed by our pious ancestors.

"1644.

"Ordered, that twoe be appointed every Lord's day, to walk forth in the time of God's worshippe, to tak notice of such as either lye about the meeting-house, without attending to the word or ordinances, or that lye at home, or in the fields, without giving good account thereof, and to tak the names of such persons, and to present them to the magistrate, whereby they may be accordingly proceeded against."

"1677.

"Whereas, there hath been several complaints of several persons that doe profane the Sabbath, by unseasonable walking abroad even at the time of publique service, andc.—the Selectmen have agreed each of them to take their turns, with the constables to walk abroad on the Lord's day, both forenoon and afternoone, morning and evening, to redress such miscarriages as they shall at any time meet withal."

But the following license granted by the selectmen in 1672, shows a much greater liberality than is exhibited in these days.

"1672.

"Nathaniel Ingerson is allowed to sell beer and syder by the quart, for the tyme whyle the farmers are a building of their meeting-house, and on Lord's days afterwards."

Salem Observer, July 14, 1827.

The interest, which is now felt in the subject of the Sabbath, renders the following article, respecting the curiosity of Le Sage, worthy the attention of the reader. It was extracted from a review of Le Sage, published in Scotland about twelve years ago.

"At the time we are now speaking of the Sabbath was observed at Geneva, with a gloom and austerity of which we, in Scotland can probably form a more correct notion than the inhabitants of any other country in Christendom. Le Sage felt some curiosity to know whether the author of Nature still continued to impose on himself the same law that originally marked the institution of the day of rest. It would have puzzled the first philosopher in Europe to think of any method by which this question could be brought to the decision of experiment: but the ingenuity of our young enquirer soon suggested an experiment.—He measured, with great care, the increase of a plant day after day, in order to discover whether it would cease growing on the Sabbath. The result could not fail to solve the difficulty, and to convince the young man, that though the work of Creation might terminate, the work of Providence is never interrupted."

Salem Observer, 1829.

Sunday in Salem in 1838.

SALEM AND THE SABBATH.

On our way to church in the quiet city of Salem recently, a stranger overtook us, and inquired where the Rev. Mr. W—— was to preach that morning? We answered that we were going to his church, and would show him a seat. For which he expressed his thanks and immediately remarked, that he had travelled recently nearly over all our country, and nowhere had he witnessed such entire abandonment of all secular avocations on the Sabbath. It seemed like a different country, and made him feel the significance of the name of that ancient town—Salem, City of Peace.—Christian (Boston) Monitor.

Fifty years ago hardly any one thought of absenting himself or herself from public worship. People went to church as a matter of course, partly from a sense of duty, and partly from habit; and this is still the case to some extent. The majority of thoughtful persons of all religious persuasions are agreed upon one point, and that is, it is desirable to have Sunday set apart as a day of rest and change from the ordinary cares and business of life. From a sanitary point of view this rest is no doubt of the highest importance. All people, moreover, who desire to have quiet for religious worship should at least not be disturbed. Public opinion ought to be protection enough; but unfortunately it might not be, so that laws to such an extent as is necessary for this purpose should be in force. But the idea entertained by certain fanatics, that no one should walk or ride for health and recreation, or even engage in any innocent occupation, on Sunday, is so absurd as not to deserve a moment's consideration.

In 1829 a futile attempt was made to put a stop to the delivery of Sunday mails, one result of which was the holding of a number of public meetings in Salem, the reports of which we take from the papers.

Meetings were also held in Boston and New York.

PUBLIC MEETING.

At a very numerous and respectable meeting of the citizens of Salem, "opposed to Legislative interference in respect to the religious observances of Sunday," held at the Town Hall, Dec. 27, 1828, Perley Putnam, Esq., was called to the chair, and Dr. Benjamin Kittredge, appointed Secretary.—The object of the meeting having been stated by the Chairman, it was

Voted, That Messrs. George Cleveland, Leverett Saltonstall, Stephen C. Phillips, John W. Treadwell, Perley Putnam, Nath'l West, jun., Franklin H. Story, John Crowninshield, Jos. G. Waters, Charles A. Andrew, David Pingree, and David A. Neal, be a committee[2] to consider and report at an adjournment of the meeting, what measures it is expedient to take for the purpose of carrying into effect the objects of the meeting.

The meeting was then adjourned for one week.

[2] The committee appointed consisted of Episcopalians, Unitarians, and Universalists.

At the adjourned meeting on Saturday evening Jan. 3, 1829, the Committee reported the following Resolutions, which were unanimously adopted:—

Resolved, That the observance of Sunday as a day of religious worship and instruction is eminently adapted to extend the knowledge and influence of truth and virtue, and thus to improve the character and increase the happiness of individuals and of the community.

Resolved, That under no circumstances has religion excited such general interest, as when, not rendered odious by legal restraints, it has addressed its claims for support to the understandings and consciences of men.

Resolved, That a "system of regulations" for the purpose of enforcing religious observances is opposed to the principles of religious liberty and to our form of civil government; and it is to be feared that any attempts to introduce such regulations will re-act in consequences detrimental to the interests which it may have been intended to promote.

Resolved, That neither the precepts of Christianity nor the design of religious observances are incompatible with the prompt and faithful discharge of the various duties which belong to our social and civil relations; and the urgency of such duties may frequently render it of importance to every individual to receive or transmit intelligence with the least possible delay.

Resolved, That for the necessary accommodation of the Government and citizens of this widely extended country, an arrangement of the mails, by which letters and packages are forwarded and delivered with the utmost despatch and safety, has been for a great length of time maintained under the vigilant superintendence of the Postmaster General; and such arrangement, while it is productive of innumerable advantages to the Government and to the citizens, is not allowed to interfere with the public religious services on Sunday.[B]

Resolved, That any change in the present arrangement of the mails which shall have the effect to subject to increased delay and hazard the communication between distant parts of the country is impolitic; and if authorized by Congress for the sole purpose of enforcing religious observances, will be an exercise of power for the accomplishment of an object not recognized by the Constitution, and contrary to its spirit and the intentions of its framers.

Resolved, That if Congress should prohibit the forwarding of mails and the delivery of letters on Sunday, individuals and the Government will be obliged to resort to such temporary arrangements for transmitting intelligence as their respective exigencies may require; and such temporary arrangements, while they will be attended with increased expense, will be productive of far greater inconvenience and disturbance to the religious public, than can justly be complained of under the present system.

Resolved, That a committee be appointed, who shall be instructed to prepare a memorial to Congress expressive of the views of this meeting, whenever in their opinion, circumstances shall render it expedient to present such memorial; and such memorial shall be submitted by them for approbation, at a meeting to be called for that purpose.

Resolved, That the committee appointed in conformity to the foregoing resolution, shall be authorized to call future meetings, to correspond with citizens of other towns, and generally to take such measures as they may deem expedient for the purpose of carrying into effect the objects of this meeting.

The following gentlemen were appointed a committee to perform the duties specified in the two last resolutions, viz. George Cleveland, Dudley L. Pickman, Willard Peele, Perley Putnam, Philip Chase, Stephen White, Gideon Tucker, Nath'l Frothingham, Stephen C. Phillips. The Committee was authorized to fill any vacancies that may occur in their number.

Voted, That an attested copy of the proceedings be published in the several newspapers in this town, and in one or more of the newspapers in the city of Washington, and that an attested copy be also forwarded to the Post Master General.

The meeting was then dissolved.

PERLEY PUTNAM, Chairman.

Benj. Kittredge, Secretary.

[B] Extract from Regulations respecting Post Offices.—"At Post Offices where the mail arrives on Sunday, the office is to be kept open for the delivery of letters, andc. for one hour or more after the arrival and assorting of the mail; but in case that would interfere with the hours of public worship, then the office is to be kept open for one hour after the usual time of dissolving the meeting for that purpose."

A very large meeting of citizens of New York, opposed to the proposition to discontinue the mails on Sunday, was held at New York this week. A similar meeting has also been held at Boston.

SABBATH MAILS.

Salem, (Mass.) Feb. 9, 1829.

To the Hon. Richard M. Johnson, Chairman of the Committee on the Post

Office and Post Roads, Washington.

Sir:—The subscribers, a committee appointed at a meeting of the inhabitants of this town, on the 3d January last, to take such measures as they may deem expedient to oppose any attempts to interfere for religious purposes with the transportation of the Mails and opening the Post Offices on Sunday, have read with pleasure the report of the Committee of the Senate on that subject.

Previous to receiving that report, they were about petitioning Congress—and the public sentiment in this place is so universal against an interference for religious reasons, that a very respectable and numerous subscription could readily have been obtained.—But the report from the Senate represented the subject in so powerful a light—demonstrated so clearly the want of power in the government to legislate for the reasons given by the petitioners, and showed so conclusively, that if they had the power, they certainly had not the ability to determine for all the people of the United States, what God's law was—that we have concluded it would not be necessary at the present session of Congress to take any further steps in the business. We have thought, however, that tho' constituting but a small part of the United States, yet it might not be uninteresting to the committee, to know how much in accordance with our views are the sentiments expressed in their report and to assure them for ourselves, and those whom we represent, that we shall at all times consider them engaged in the highest and most momentous acts of legislation, whenever their efforts shall tend to prevent an interference of the religious with the civil power—all union between church and state—all attempts of religious zealots to enforce by law, what they may term divine truth.

You will please to convey to the gentlemen of the committee, our sense of their proceedings, and for yourself, sir, accept the assurance of our respectful consideration.

GEORGE CLEVELAND,
GIDEON TUCKER,
DUDLEY L. PICKMAN,
WILLARD PEELE,
PERLEY PUTNAM,
NATHANIEL FROTHINGHAM.

The following item is from the "Observer" of Jan. 21, 1829:—

The Report of the Senate on the Sunday Mails. The Portsmouth Advertiser has attacked this Report, "tooth and nail," imputing to it an influence as disastrous as that which attends the writings of Tom Paine or Citizen Brisset. The writer states, that the Senate by adopting it, "has virtually declared, that the laws of Almighty God are no rule for human legislation." We will give one more extract from these remarks, to enable our readers to form a judgment of the writer's character. He must certainly belong to that unfortunate class of the community, for whom "strait-jackets and a spare diet," are usually prescribed.

"By this report, Col. Johnson has put weapons into the hands of infidelity to annoy and harass that very portion of the republican community, which furnishes the only hope, and pledge, that our free institutions will continue permanent."

The following account of a Parisian Sabbath we find in the "Salem Observer" of 1830:

Parisian Sabbath. There is little in the appearance of Paris on a Sabbath morning to remind us that it is a day of rest; the markets are thronged as on other days, carts and drays and all sorts of vehicles, designed for the transportation of merchandise are in motion; buying and selling and manual labor proceed as usual; there is rest for neither man nor beast. In the afternoon the shops are usually closed; and labor is suspended, and the remainder of the day is devoted to pleasure. Few of those who go to church appear to have any other motive than amusement. They walk about the aisles, gazing at the pictures, and listening to the solemn music of the mass and go away when they are tired. Those whom I have seen really engaged in worship appeared to belong to the lower classes; and with the exception of those few, the persons you see in church are merely idle spectators, attracted thither by curiosity, or to pass an idle half hour before they go to promenade in the gardens.

—Wheaton's Travels.

In the "Salem Observer" of Dec. 10, 1829, is the following notice on the Sunday-mail question:—

Sunday Mails. The following resolution on the subject of stopping the mails on Sundays, was passed at a recent session of the Salem Baptist Association in Kentucky:—

"Resolved, That we as an Association cordially approve the Report and resolution, as presented to the Senate of the United States, by Col. R.M. Johnson, Chairman of the Committee upon the subject of the petition to stop the mail on the Sabbath: and sincerely advise all friends of civil and religious liberty, to refuse to subscribe any petition that has the least tendency to influence the legislative powers to act upon religious matters; for we consider an association of civil and ecclesiastical power or an union of Church and State, as one of the greatest calamities which could befal our country, and that it should be resisted in every possible shape in which it may be presented."

A great change has taken place in some of our towns within a few years in reference to the Sunday mail. Twenty-five years ago it was rare to see a person belonging to one of the Evangelical sects at the post-office at the time of the opening of the mail on Sunday noon; whereas now it is not uncommon to see deacons and numerous other members of such churches hurry from their several places of worship to get their letters and papers with as much eagerness as "heretics." Sunday papers moreover are now bought by the same class. The same change too is observable in the use of horse-cars on Sunday. Few men are governed by the conscientious scruples once held about riding to and from church, especially if the day happens to be hot or stormy. This may or may not be an improvement; it depends upon the point of view from which we look at it.

One of the most radical men we ever knew, one who thought "Sunday should be abolished" and a "new Bible made by men of modern ideas, and reasonable views introduced, and the old one discarded," said he was brought to these views by having been forced when young to attend church and engage in religious exercises, and told that he must conform to the established belief and never ask any questions. It will be said that this man was an exception to the general rule. Perhaps so, for one taking such an extreme view; but we must all know cases somewhat similar. A careful inquiry will show that if we look around among the clergy even, we shall find that the most radical preachers of the day were brought up in the Orthodox ranks. Who would wish to re-establish the gloomy Puritan Sabbath, with its barren meeting-house, without fires or music, and its tedious, uninteresting sermon, running on to "fifteenthly," gauged by an hour-glass turned over perhaps once or twice during the discourse?

Speaking of the change of habits in New England, even, it is noticeable how much more prevalent colds and other slight indispositions are now to what they used to be on Sunday. The very thought of going to church makes some people cough or have a headache. Theatres or concerts never seem to affect these people in the same way. Even the weather, which keeps people in-doors on Sunday, never keeps them in on other days.

Our own view of the subject is that while we should be glad to see more interest taken in public worship than there is at present, we think people should have the right of spending their Sundays in their own way,—always, of course, provided they do not interfere with the rights and feelings of others. It seems to us that the only way to have Sunday properly observed is for those who are influential to make some little personal sacrifices, if need be, to attend the Sunday services, and do all they can to promote the most cheerful views of religion and make the services interesting.

Let those people who lament the decay of religious observances read the following quotation from the "Salem Gazette" of 1830. Those who can recollect how it was at that date must see that notwithstanding a perhaps much smaller attendance now upon public worship, there is every reason to believe that, at least as far as the native population is concerned, Sunday is really more quiet than it was then. After reading this article we shall perhaps be prepared to say that "tythingmen" may have been needed just after the Revolution.

The Times we live in. The dreadful tragedy performed in this town last April, and the subsequent arrests, developments, confessions, trials, andc., by keeping the thoughts and conversation of the community continually directed to that enormity, have led to the general but very erroneous notion, that there must have been a great deterioration of the public morals.—If the words of the aged are to be received as true, the very reverse is the fact. The revolutionary war left the whole country as well depraved in morals as exhausted in resources. This was particularly the case with such towns as Salem, which had been largely exposed to the irresistibly corrupting influence of privateering.

At that time, when the population of Salem was not half so great as it is at present, more riot, debauchery, and vice, obtruded themselves upon the sight in a week, than could now be discovered by diligent search in a month. The corruption of manners was so general, that almost none escaped from its contaminating influence. Mechanics and other laboring men would leave their business in the day, and their families in the evening, to spend their time, dancing and drinking, in the dens of pollution which then abounded in "Naugus-Hole" and "Button-Hole." Merchants, professional men, andc. passed a great part of their time in taverns, drinking and gambling. Quarrelling and fighting there were not uncommon, and well-worn packs of cards were always lying about the bar-room tables, (though seldom long unemployed,) ready for the use of visitors,—the common game on these occasions being All-Fours, and the common stake a bowl of punch or a mug of flip. Pastimes like the above named, were current in every class of society. When the regular hours of drinking approached, the workmen left their labour to play at cards, the loser "treating the shop's crew." In a large establishment a boy would be kept running with his jug nearly the whole time, the contents being freely shared amongst master, journeymen, boys, and numerous visitors.

At this time, and long afterward, infamous houses were kept open day and night, in the quarters of the town named in the preceding paragraph. The fiddles were kept in constant motion, and if any thought of stopping them they did not dare to attempt it. The most flagrant disorders and outrages were continually occurring, so that a timid man would go far out of his way to avoid passing near those places. The churches on Sunday were not nearly so well attended as they now are. The proportion of persons who made the Sabbath a day of recreation, was much greater. The time was spent in riding into the country, walking about the fields and pastures, and visiting friends in town. But little order was preserved in the streets on that day. People in passing to meeting thro' Prison Lane, (as County-street was then called) and its environs, encountered frequent and large groups of men and boys, noisily engaged in gambling with props, pitching coppers, andc. occasionally enlivened by the uproar of a quarrel.

The doctrines of Tom Paine and his French coadjutors, were much more in vogue then than now. Infidelity stalked over the land with a giant stride, to which the mincing pace of the fooleries of Fanny Wright can bear no comparison; and virtue and good order were almost put out of countenance. Intemperance, habitual or occasional, was so common, as to be hardly considered a matter of reproach; and the kindred vices abounded, which usually follow in its train.

The state of society has been continually improving since. The bad habits of that time have been discarded one after another, by all who would maintain a reputable standing; and open immorality now places a man at once in the lowest rank of society. Intemperance has been diminished in a surprising degree. Debauchery has been compelled to retreat to lurking holes and corners, instead of obtruding its "horrid front" to the public gaze. Education has been improved, and universally diffused; and public worship is more generally attended.—Terrible crimes have indeed been committed amongst us, and may be again, but the habits and manners which lead to crime, are less prevalent at the present time than they have been for fifty years before.

It seems to us to be clearly a mistake for those of ultra-liberal notions to suppose that all who cannot assent to their views of Sunday must of necessity be either Pharisees or hypocrites,—quite as great a mistake as that of the ultra-conservatives, who condemn as wicked all who do not believe in a puritanical observance of Sunday.

Whatever we may think or say or do, people nowadays will not be forced to attend church. Among all denominations the services are more attractive than they once were, and every year there is less and less of the repulsive kinds of doctrine preached. But in spite of this, while many men regard attendance on divine service as both a pleasure and a privilege, there are others, and they not few, whom no influence or persuasion can induce to attend Sunday worship. Such persons must be left to spend the day as they please.

A very large proportion of those who do not attend church services are people of culture and character, from whom church-goers have nothing to fear as regards a disturbance of their worship. Generally this class are interested in having Sunday kept as a day of quiet and rest, and their non-attendance at church is no evidence that they have any desire to secularize Sunday.

An eminent writer has said: "We live in a transition period, when the old faiths which comforted nations, and not only so, but made nations, seem to have spent their force.... There is faith in chemistry, in meat and wine, in wealth, in machinery, in the steam-engine, galvanic battery, turbine-wheels, sewing-machines, and in public opinion; but not in divine causes.... A silent revolution has loosed the tension of the old religious sects, and in place of the gravity and permanence of those societies of opinion, they run into freak and extravagance.... In creeds never was such levity: witness the heathenisms in Christianity,—the periodic revivals, the millennium mathematics, the peacock ritualism, the retrogression to popery, the maundering of Mormons, the squalor of mesmerism, the deliration of rappings, the rat-and-mouse revelation, thumps in table-drawers, and black art ... By the irresistible maturing of the general mind the Christian traditions have lost their hold."

If these statements are true, we have a sufficient answer to the question so often asked: "Why do not people go to church as they once did?" They do not go because they have lost their faith in churches and worship,—at least such have as are appealed to from those holding liberal and reasonable views. There are no doubt men who consider the too often expensive ways in which churches are supported as altogether beyond their means. The demands of civilization upon individuals in these restless times, when there are so many organizations, secret, secular, and religious, are indeed too great for small incomes, especially as the cost of food is continually increasing, and as society in other ways makes so many secular demands upon them. Public worship is after all, in the view of many persons, not a necessity, but only a luxury which can easily be dispensed with. It might perhaps have been better for the whole community if churches had undertaken to do the work which is now in the hands of many charitable and secret societies; then those who take so much interest in these outside, often expensive, organizations would have had all their interest in the churches. But the latter were for years so divided on doctrines of belief that their whole attention has for the most part been directed to other matters than their legitimate work, which has thus been thrown into the hands of outside agencies. In these times it seems difficult to maintain religious societies except where the element of fear is dominant in the creed, where some remarkable preacher takes the attention, or where the ritual or fashion attracts. Do not the papers often speak of "fashionable" churches?

One thing which prevents many people from attending public worship on Sunday is the increasing tendency towards ritualism,—or perhaps, we should say, making the services less instructive than formerly, and more devotional or emotional. This is seen not only in the Episcopal Church, but also among many other denominations. Even Congregational Orthodox— descendants of the Pilgrim Fathers—introduce prayer-books and responsive services, and make their church buildings more ecclesiastical in appearance, to look as much as possible like Episcopal churches. All these things to many minds are not edifying, to say the least, and consequently such persons absent themselves from service. Those too who are impressed by emotional religion join the Episcopalians, so that for the time there is an apparent increase in the attendance at the Episcopal churches, gained from churches of other denominations; and especially too as fashion decrees nowadays that "it is the proper thing to do" to go to the Episcopal Church, whether you believe in its doctrines or not. So that at length there are a great many people who think when church-going gets to be a matter of fashion, there is quite as much real religion to be found outside as inside the church; consequently they lose their interest. All these causes must be taken together; of course no one thing alone accounts for the change in regard to church attendance.

We quote the following remarks from a recent English paper ("The Unitarian Herald"); they have a direct bearing on our subject, and are worthy of consideration by those who neglect public worship or favor a more secular Sunday. Among other things, the speaker (the Rev. John Page Hopps) says:

"So far as we can see, the old orthodox believers were right when they called public worship 'a means of grace;' and if human experience is of any value, it is an undoubted fact that a great multitude which no man could number have felt the grace-giving influence of it. It is as true as ever that man cannot 'live by bread alone,' but that he needs also the 'word that proceedeth from the mouth of God;' and if it is true, as we believe, that the word of God does come home with special force and pathos when worship is joined in by kindred souls, the argument for public worship, from this point of view, seems complete. And yet, half in jest and half in earnest, and sometimes altogether in earnest, we hear it said that a man can worship God in the fields quite as well as in the church. 'Perhaps he can,' said a wise man once, 'but does he?' I wonder whether we shall go on in this direction until we hear it said that a man can worship God playing at lawn-tennis as in attending public worship? Thus there may actually come into existence a cant of the absentee which shall be as really cant as the cant of the devotee; for the use of the word 'worship' in such instances is a glaring case of exaggeration tinged with self-deception, which is the very essence of cant. Besides, one of the surest notes of the worshipping spirit is an increase of sympathy and love,—sympathy that suggests fellowship, and love that suggests anything but selfish isolation.

"The irregularity also of attendance upon public worship might be cited as an instance of neglect or levity which 'personal consecration' alone can cure. In days gone by, attendance upon public worship was a habit, and nothing that could be avoided was allowed to interfere with it. Twice on the Sunday, too, was the rule, and not, as now, the decided exception. But with many it is now becoming once every other Sunday, or scarcely that; with so little of 'personal consecration' in the matter that the need for an umbrella may decide the doubter not to go.

"Do we not, again, listen too much merely for delight? and does not the question, 'How did you like the sermon,' or 'How did you like the service,' indicate that we join in the service and listen to a sermon in an entirely wrong spirit? The critical or self-regarding spirit has its uses, but it may be fatal to 'personal consecration' in public worship. How often does an entire service depend upon our own temper, our own mood, our own spirit? And how often is it true that a congregation has as much to do with the making of a minister as the minister has to do with the making of a congregation?

"'If I neglect public worship, then,' a man should say to himself, 'the community is injured, the brotherhood is weakened, the young are confused. It is a grave responsibility.'

"But now we must not shrink from the question: How far or how long ought these considerations to hold the man who has lost delight in public worship or faith in that to which it bears witness? When should doubt make worship impossible, or unbelief make worship wrong for the honest soul? When should 'personal consecration' say to a man, not stay, but depart? It is a grave question, and every one must shape his answer for himself. All I would say is: Give worship the benefit of the doubt: ay! give fellow-worshippers the benefit of the doubt. Continue with them as long as you can; if not as a full believer, then as a devout inquirer, a gentle seeker, a sympathetic friend. Why not? That is possible with us; for the very bond of our union is sympathetic regard for one another's freedom. It is also specially possible with us because our teachings do not, at all events, outrage the reason and shock the moral sense. Even an agnostic might listen to us and hope that our Gospel is true.

"Special dangers call for special safeguards, special consideration, special wariness. It is an age of splendid advance in science, of restless energy in business, of stupendous activity in politics, of daring questioning everywhere. All that makes against public worship; and yet all that makes public worship a greater necessity and demonstrates 'the pressing need of personal consecration' to it. God only knows what we should do without it and the blessed Sunday!

"'Dear old commemorative day,
For weary man designed
To help him on life's troubled way,
To give his spirit freer play,
To soothe his harassed mind!
"'A day of worship and of grace,
One calm, sweet day in seven,
To grant a little breathing space
To strengthen man life's work to face,
And lift his life to heaven.'"

In conclusion, let us add to the above speech the following remarks, which we heartily approve,—

"Mr. Preston (London) testified to the falling off of attendance at public worship, and he attributed this largely to the parents not taking their children with them in early years, as of old times. He deprecated the going to public worship to have the brains tickled in hearing a particular man, and maintained that this was in no sense 'public worship.' He emphasized strongly the fact that those who say they can worship in the fields do not, in fact, worship at all. He urged that in worship the musical and devotional services should become more prominent, and the sermon become frequently but subsidiary."

www.ingramcontent.com/pod-product-compliance
Lightning Source LLC
Chambersburg PA
CBHW061936280526
45787CB00004B/1628